New Start Suspense Series
Part 1

RESOURCE GUIDE

By Patricia Birtwistle

ISBN 0-9733663-7-0

Patnor Publishing

New Start Suspense Series Part 1

RESOURCE GUIDE

By Pat Birtwistle

ACKNOWLEDGMENTS

A heartfelt thanks to Pat Nelson, my friend and research consultant, for her help and encouragement; Nick Sidoti for his enthusiasm, wealth of ideas and insights; Ann Marie Crocco for allowing the students in her school to pilot these novelettes and her encouragement; Angela Marcov who piloted these novelettes and showed such enthusiasm, and to Dot Wishart and Mary Cordeiro for their editing skills. And a special thanks to Paul Dayboll for his help with how to best get these books printed and for creating our website.

Above all, a very special thanks to Norm, my husband and best friend, for all his hard work in making these books become a reality.

New Start Suspense Series

Part 1

RESOURCE GUIDE

Table of Contents

"This is baby stuff. I want to read a novel." Comments like this are being expressed daily by young people across the country. The dilemma is that the reader's independent or instructional reading level is at grade two or three while chronological age may be significantly higher. Reading materials at this level look like books for the six, seven or eight-year old. Parents, teachers and librarians are frustrated by the lack of high interest, low vocabulary materials. The focus in these novelettes is on
the reluctant reader, learning disabled, brain injured, those with attention deficit disorder and anyone learning English as their second language. The vocabulary is level two
and a word list is available to assist the instructor/parent in assessing the material quickly and determining its use as instructional or independent. However, it does not look like "baby stuff".

The contention of the author is that reluctant readers will begin to make progress when they experience a level of comfort with interesting, readable material.

These novelettes have not been illustrated. Illustrations, in the author's opinion, make the books appear juvenile. Also, the ages of the characters have been obscured to enable the reader to enter the stories as they wish.

The questions provided for each chapter of each book are intended to promote discussion. Some questions elicit information but most promote the growth of comprehension, evaluation and predictability skills. Developing these thinking skills should further reading abilities. The instructor/parent could easily adapt the material to further factual questions, build character studies, predict the outcomes or write book reports.

Each novelette stands alone and is not dependent on the others for content or continuity of action. The vocabulary, however, becomes progressively more difficult.
Therefore, it is recommended that readers begin with book one and continue through the series. Each chapter in each book ends with a "cliff hanger" to encourage the reader to continue reading or make predictions as to the outcomes for that chapter. This element of suspense, along with the ease of the read, will encourage interest in the series and over time, reading in general.

Chapters are short and have not been allowed to run from one page to another. These limitations allow for increased comprehension. Being able to easily complete a paragraph, a page, or a chapter, at this stage, is a rewarding experience.

These non-threatening suspense stories have been piloted with a group of young people ages ten to eighteen and have been met with great enthusiasm. A librarian at a local library described this series as filling a "black hole in literature".

The Principal and the Resource Teacher from the piloted school were both enthusiastic and relieved that a series of books would be published to meet this existent need in schools. Their claim was that there are a number of ways that these very unique books could be used within their classrooms. The students who took part in the pilot project were described as "hating school, hating reading and experiencing behavioral problems". Once they began the first novelette they were "begging" the resource teacher to "take us for reading today."

About the Author

Patricia Birtwistle was a teacher and consultant of Special Education for most of her career. One of her biggest challenges was finding appropriate reading materials for the many and varied student learning needs within the boundaries of her jurisdiction.

After being retired for a number of years, Patricia was asked to find some reading materials for a sixteen-year old brain injured young man. She searched libraries, bookstores and catalogues to no avail. It was then that Patricia began writing this series and she looks forward to seeing them in the hands of many young people who need or want to read.

Objectives

To fill the gap in the literary field by providing high interest, low vocabulary novelettes for reluctant readers, English as a Second Language students, the brain injured and the learning disabled.

Education B.A. - University of Western Ontario (1968) Specialist in Special Education Principal Certificate

Experience

Elementary School Teacher
Teacher of Elementary Grades - Middlesex County Roman Catholic School Board

Taught grades 7 and 8

Principal of School

Special Education Teacher - Welland County Separate School Board

General Learning Disabilities Class (ages 10-14) Specific Learning Disabilities Class (ages 10-14)

Liaison Teacher for Special Education - Welland County Separate School Board.

 Assisted Teachers/Parents in locating materials for Special Education students in the segregated classes

Assessed needs of students Programming assistance for Teachers

Student Services Consultant - Welland County Separate School Board

Programming assistance for Teachers
    Team Leader of Student Services Group consisting of a Psychologist, Speech
    Pathologist, Teacher for the Gifted, Resource Teacher and Diagnostician

Overview of Novelettes

New Start Suspense Series revolves around five young people who find themselves in and out of trouble all summer. Some vocabulary is taken from the "Most
Frequently Used Word List". These words are reinforced throughout the series and other vocabulary is added as needed but is controlled and repeated for reader comfort.

The chapters are short and end with "cliff hangers" or conflict. The story in each of the novelettes takes place over one or two days and are filled with adventure.

As previously stated, the targeted audience is mainly the reluctant reader, those studying English as a Second Language, the brain injured, those with Attention Deficit Disorder and the learning disabled, but this does not preclude their use in other venues.

Book Outlines

Book One: "The Swamp"

Two of the characters find a locked bag beside a skeletal hand wearing a ruby ring. As they investigate, they are trapped behind falling rocks. The remainder of the book revolves around whether they will be rescued and what they should do about the locked bag, ring and hand.

Book Two: "The Old House"

An old house is located in the swamp and is rumored to be haunted. The young people decide to enter the house. At one point, they hear what they think is a cry of someone in trouble but are uncertain if the cry is that of a child, a ghost, someone in the house or simply the wind. Their resulting actions put them in trouble with their parents.

Book Three: "What A Day"

A day at the lake sounds innocent enough. Beth almost drowns, Bob attempts a rescue and Nick saves the life of a little girl and her father. Once again the parents are distraught to discover that their children's adventures have led them into dangerous territory.

Book Four: "The Junk Yard"

Kim, always trying to get rich, decides to go to the junk yard alone to look for treasures. The owner is not there and has left his dog out in the yard to guard it. Kim is trapped on top of a pile of junk when the dog discovers her. No one knows where Kim is.

Book Five: "The Trip"

The parents are reluctant to allow the kids to go on an all-day horseback riding trip, but eventually give in. While the kids are waiting their turn to ride, they encounter a poisonous snake in a pool of water. They are afraid to move and decide that they must kill the snake or be killed by it.

When they are finally out riding, the horses are spooked and the Lead Hand is not there. Beth must stop the stampede before someone gets badly hurt.

Book Six: "At The Mall"

The group is doing their back to school shopping. Kim finds a bag with a large amount of money in it. She is conflicted about keeping it or turning it in. The others convince her to turn it in. However, a stranger has seen her with the money and follows the kids the entire day.

Getting Started

Enjoyment in reading these novelettes is of primary importance. Therefore, the same steps used in choosing a novel should be followed here. These skills will benefit readers in their future choice of books.

Suggested discussion could be:

• What is the title of the novelette? What does it tell you about the book?

• The artist's creation on the cover also reveals something about the book? What can you tell about the book by the cover?

- Read the description on the back cover. What does the author tell you to make you want to read this book?

- Someone has read this book and tells something about it. How does what they say make you want to read it?

<u>Discussion Questions</u>

The discussion questions are designed for use following each chapter. The reader can be encouraged to think about the events in that chapter and elaborate on their thinking.

The Swamp

Chapter One - The Swamp

- Why do you think the kids liked going to the swamp?
- What will Kim do with the ring if she gets it?
- If you were Nick or Kim, what would you do?

Chapter Two – Trapped

- What else is in the spot besides the hand and the bag?
- How do you think the hand and bag got there?
- What do you think will come next?

Chapter Three – Help

- Why shouldn't Dan leave Nick and Kim?
- Should Dan go for help? Explain.
- What two things could kill Nick and Kim? Can you think of some others?

Chapter Four – The Pact

- Should the kids have told Nick's mom? Why or why not?
- Why did they have to get out of the swamp before the sun set?
- Did the kids do the best thing by not telling their folks? Why do you think that?

Chapter Five - What To Do

- What happened to the hand?
- Have you ever made a pact? When?
- Would your folks get mad if you were Nick or Kim? Why?

The Old House

Chapter One - The Old House

- Would you be afraid to go to the old house? Why?
- What kind of person is Beth?
- Why do you think the trunk is locked?

Chapter Two - The Cry

- Should the kids have gone back for Beth? Why?
- Why do you think the old man locked the trunk?
- What do you think is making the crying sound?

Chapter Three - Back To The House

- Would you go upstairs if you were one of the kids? Why or why not?
- What riches could be in the old house?
- Who do you think is in the house?

Chapter Four - Blood Tracks

- Can you think of a better plan than the one the kids had?
- If it is not a kid in the house, what could be making an adult cry?
- What do you think is next to the wall?

Chapter Five - Do Not Go Into The Swamp

- How did Beth's dad know that the kids were in trouble?
- Why do you think Ted was not afraid of the bats and rats?
- What do you think Beth's dad will do to punish the kids for going to the old house?

What A Day

Chapter One - The Best Day Yet

- Why do you think Bob was not with the rest of the kids at the swamp and the old house?
- In what ways do your parents still treat you like a little kid?
- Why does the water look so black?

Chapter Two - Beth's Trouble

- Tell how to pump someone's lungs if they were drowning?
- How is Nick feeling as Beth lay there on the raft?
- What is the stuff out on the lake?

Chapter Three - Will He Make It

- How was Nick feeling as he swam out to the stuff on the lake?
- Will Nick find the man?
- If Nick finds the man, can you think of ways he could get him back on the mast?

Chapter Four - What To Do

- Can you think of other ways the kids could have made it out to help Nick?
- Did Bob do the right thing by trying to swim out to Nick? Why?
- What are they going to do now?

Chapter Five - What A Day

- Why didn't Nick yell back?
- How did Nick get the man on to the mast?
- Do the kids look for trouble or does trouble find them? Explain.

The Junk Yard

Chapter One - Keep Out

- Describe in detail what you think the dog looked like.
- Why do you think Kim went the back way into the junkyard?
- What should Kim do?

Chapter Two - Kim's Not Here

- What kind of kid is Dan?
- Kim's mom is upset. What would you do if you were Kim's mom?
- What will Beth do when she does not find Kim by the rock?

Chapter Three - Back At The Junk Yard

- If Kim had not fallen and kept talking softly, do you think the dog would have let her go?
- How do you feel about the dog?
- What will the dog do to Kim?

Chapter Four - Where's Kim

- Do you know people who are competitive like Dan and Bob? Describe them.
- Where do you go to be by yourself?
- What will the kids do when they get to the junkyard?

Chapter Five - Stay Out

- Why does the man keep kids out of the junkyard?
- Why didn't the dog hurt Kim?
- What will Kim tell her mom about her day?

The Trip

Chapter One - The Trip

- Describe how Kim was feeling after her trouble at the junkyard.
- When have you pushed your parents to let you do something? Did you succeed?
- Was Dan right to try and get back at Beth? Why do you think that?

Chapter Two - At The Pool

- How was Dan planning to get back at the kids?
- Why do so many people hate snakes?
- How would you kill the snake?

Chapter Three - On The Hill

- How would you feel if you were Nick?
- Why did Beth yell?
- What will happen next?

Chapter Four - The Ride

- What words would you use to describe how the kids felt when the snake took off?
- Why didn't the farmer ask the kids why they looked upset?
- Will someone get hurt?

Chapter Five - You Can Do It

- What would you do if you were Beth? 13

• Why did the farmer not want the horses to have a lot to drink?
• What do you think they told their parents about the trip?

At The Mall

Chapter One – The Money

   • How much money do you think the kids had?
   • If you saw a "dirty little bag" in a mall, what would you do?
   • Explain "finders keepers". Do you think it is right?

Chapter Two - The Best Thing To Do

   • What would you do if you were Kim?
   • What do you think the shop owner will do with the money?
   • Why do you think the man is following the kids?

Chapter Three - The Man

   • Do you think the boys should have told their parents about the man?
   • Would you have tried to find the man? Why or why not?
   • What should Nick do?

Chapter Four - Should We Go Back

   • What would you do with all that money?
   • Which of the boy's plans do you like best and why?
   • What will happen next?

Chapter Five - Back At The Mall

   • Describe how the boys were feeling when they found that the girls had left for the mall.
   • What would you do if you were the kids' parents?
   • What did you like best about this story?

Word Lists

The Word Lists may be photocopied by the parent/instructor if the photocopying benefits the reader.

Word Lists are presented in various ways:

• The complete vocabulary list for the entire series is approximately 300-400 words.

• There is also a complete alphabetical list of all words in the series.

• These words could be used in other activities for reinforcement. Much of the vocabulary is repeated throughout the series.

The Swamp
Chapter One

Name _______________________

<u>Word Study</u> – Pick One

1) The <u>Swamp</u> is   _______

    a) a big rock

    b) a hot wet spot

    c) a locked bag

2) The big red <u>rock</u> was on a   _______

    a) ring

    b) stick

    c) bug

3) A <u>gap</u> in the rocks is a   _______

    a) a thing with no skin

    b) a spot in the rocks

    c) a hand

4) The sun was getting <u>dim.</u> That is   _______

    a) hot

    b) red

    c) going down

5) The kids lived   _______

    a) at the swamp

    b) in a cool spot

    c) on the block

Comprehension – Yes Or No

1) The hand looked like a stick. _____

2) The rest of the man was with that hand. _____

3) When the sun sets it gets cool. _____

4) The kids wanted to tell the folks. _____

5) Kim's mom would get mad. _____

Fill in the blanks   no one   the folks   Kim   Nick   the kids on the block

1) Who liked to go to the swamp? _____________________

2) Who kicked the sand by the hand? _____________________

3) Who wanted the ring? _____________________

4) Who did not want the kids to go to the swamp? _____________________

5) Who did Nick and Kim want to tell about the hand? _____________________

Character Study - Tell about

1) I think Nick is _____________________

2) Why?_____________________

Prediction

What do you think the kids will do? _____________________

____

Name ______________________

<u>Word Study</u> – Pick One

1) The kids could not <u>nod off</u>. They   ______

    a) were out

    b) at the swamp

    c) could not rest

2) There was <u>fog</u> at the swamp.   ______

    a) It was big

    b) It was a gap

    c) It was wet

3) Nick and Kim were <u>blocked</u> in. They   ______

    a) were hot

    b) could not get out

    c) were hit by rocks

4) Nick and Kim did not want to get bitten by   ______

    a) bugs

    b) fog

    c) a gap

5) A bug <u>landed</u> on Kim's hand. It   ______

    a) bit

    b) yelled

    c) stopped

<u>**Comprehension**</u> – Yes or No

The kids wanted to get the lock off the bag.   ______

Things died in the swamp.   ______

A bug went up Kim's leg.   ______

Kim hit the bug on her hand.   ______

Nick and Kim did not tell that they were going to the swamp.   ______

<u>**Fill in the blanks**</u>

Nick   Kim   the kids from the block   the folks   Nick and Kim

Who made the rocks slip?   __________________

Who did not see Nick hit the bug and kill it?   __________________

Who was upset?   __________________

Who were not at the swamp?   __________________

Who would be upset if they saw the kids at the swamp?   __________________

<u>**Character Study**</u> – Tell about

I think Kim is ____

Why do you think that? _______________________________________

____

<u>**Predictions**</u> – What do you think?

What do you think Nick and Kim should do? ____________________________

____

Name _______________________

Word Study: Pick one

1. The kids **<u>hung out</u>** in lots of spots.   ______
    a) went to
    b) looked at
    c) helped

2. Nick and Kim were **<u>trapped.</u>**   ______
    a) yelling
    b) thinking
    c) locked in

3. 3.Dan sat down to **<u>rest.</u>**   ______
    a) think
    b) stop
    c) yell

4. Dan went to a **<u>hill</u>** of rocks.   ______
    a) a big rock
    b) little rocks
    c) lots of rocks

5. Dan could not do it **<u>without</u>** help.   ______
    a) with no help
    b) with lots of help
    c) with help

Comprehension: YES or NO

1. Nick and Kim left the block when the sun was hot. _________

2. Dan went to the swamp before he went to all the spots the kids liked. _________

3. Kim and Nick wanted Dan to go for help. _________

4. Dan asked Nick and Kim to help with a big rock. _________

5. A lot of bugs came into the gap. _________

Fill-in-the-Blanks

Dan   Nick   Kim   Nick's Mom   Kim's Mom

1. Who said Nick and Kim had left before she got up? _______________________

2. Who stopped to rest on a big rock? _______________________

3. Who went for water? _______________________

4. Who said the bugs will kill them? _______________________

5. Who got one big rock out? _______________________

Character Study: Tell about

Dan is

____

I think this because ____

____

Prediction:

What do you think Dan will do?

____

____

____

Name ___________________________

Word Study: Pick one

1. Nick's mom was **cross.** ______

    a) she was upset

    b) she was mad

    c) she was bad

2. A **pact** is when ______

    a) you are all cross

    b) you are upset

    c) you all think alike

3. At **last** Nick told them ______

    a) in the end

    b) little by little

    c) not at all

4. A **jug** of water is ______

    a) a little water

    b) no water

    c) lots of water

5. **Sunset** is when the sun is ______

    a) coming up

    b) going down

    c) black

Comprehension: YES or NO

1. Beth wanted to go to the swamp. _________

2. Dan wanted to tell Nick's mom where Nick was. _________

3. A lot of kids went to help with the rocks. _________

4. The kids ran as fast as they could to the swamp. _________

5. The kids said they would come back the next day. _________

Fill-in-the-Blank

The kids   Nick   Beth   Dan

1. Who got a jug of water? _________________

2. Who ran when the bugs came out of the gap? _________________

3. Who asked for water? _________________

4. Who did not want to tell the kids about the hand and ring? _________________

5. Who made a pact? _________________

Character Study

What can you tell about Beth? ____

Why do you think that? ____

____

Prediction

What will the kids do the next day?

____

____

Name _______________________________

Word Study: Pick one

1. They **<u>wanted</u>** to get going.   ______

    a) had to

    b) would like to

    c) would not like to

2. The kids wanted to be **<u>rich.</u>**   ______

    a) be on TV

    b) wanted no money

    c) wanted lots of money

3. They want to **<u>get rid of</u>** the bag.   ______

    a) get the lock off

    b) get it back to the block

    c) get it off their hands

4. **<u>Cops</u>** are   ______

    a) folk that help

    b) folk that do not help

    c) all the kids' folks

5. To be **<u>okay</u>** with what is said is to   ______

    a) not like it

    b) like it

    c) be mad at it

Comprehension: YES or NO

1. Beth wanted to get the bag to her dad. _________

2. Beth's dad was mad when he got the bag. _________

3. The kid's were on TV the next day. _________

4. The bag had things that the bank wanted. _________

5. The kids kept the pact and did not tell what they did. _________

Fill-in-the-Blanks

Nick's Mom   The Bank   The cops   Kim   Beth

1. Who kept going back to the swamp? _________________

2. Who would have asked what was up? _________________

3. Who took the bag to the cops? _________________

4. Who wanted the bag back? _________________

5. Who wanted to get rich? _________________

Character Study

What do you think of Beth's dad?

____

Why?

____

Prediction

What mess do you think the kids will get into at the old house?

____

The Old House
Chapter One

Name ______________________________

Word Study: Pick one

1. Things smell **musty.** ______

   a) Wet and bad

   b) Spooky

   c) Hot

2. Nick **tripped.** ______

   a) Yelled

   b) Stopped

   c) Fell a little

3. The **trunk** had a lock. ______

   a) A little box

   b) A lunch box

   c) A big box

4. The bats **swooped.** ______

   a) Hung from the roof

   b) Went up and down

   c) Stopped

5. Nick's dad had a lot of **tools.** ______

   a) Things in the water

   b) Things to help with work

   c) Things that are black

Comprehension: YES or NO

1. The kids were at the old house when the sun was setting. _________

2. Bats hung from the roof of the room. _________

3. Beth was looking at the bugs running up and down the walls. _________

4. The kids wanted to go for lunch. _________

5. Beth wanted to get back to the swamp with the kids. _________

Fill-in-the-Blanks

a locked trunk   boot   the old house   the wind   cracks in the wall

1. The setting is _________________.

2. What did the kids find in the house? _________________

3. What made the house "spooky"? _________________

4. Nick tripped on a _________________.

5. The sun came in by the _________________.

Character Study

What was the old man like?

____

____

I think that because

____

____

Prediction

What will they find in the trunk?

____

____

Name ___________________________

Word Study: Pick one

1. Beth did not want to be **left out.**   ______

   a. At the rock
   b. Sick
   c. Not with the kids

2. There could be **riches** in the trunk.   ______

   a. Musty stuff
   b. Stuff to make you rich
   c. Tools

3. A crash came from **upstairs.**   ______

   a. The top of a door
   b. Top of the house
   c. Dim stairs

4. The wind was **picking up.**   ______

   a. Getting in the house
   b. Getting cool
   c. Getting fast

5. The sun was **dim**.   ______

   a. Getting red
   b. Going down
   c. Getting blacker

Comprehension: YES or NO

1. The kids got the lock off. ________

2. A crash came from upstairs. ________

3. Beth's mom said that Beth was sick. ________

4. There were riches in the trunk. ________

5. The cry was like a kid crying. ________

Fill-in-the-Blank

rain   door   trunk   up   tools

1. Nick had his dad's ________________.
2. The tools and rags were in the old man's ________________.
3. The wind was getting ________________.
4. The kid did not shut the ________________.
5. They ran when the ________________ came down fast.

Character Study

"The kids felt badly". They felt badly because Beth was not with them. This tells you that

the kids were

____

because____

Predictions

Do you think the kids' folks will find out that they were at the old house?

____

Why do you think that?

____

The Old House
Chapter Three

Name _______________________

Word Study: Pick one

1. What is a **spook**?   _______

    a. A big track

    b. A little track

    c. A man that died and has come back

2. At dusk the sun is going   _______

    a. old

    b. up

    c. down

3. Nick went softly up the steps. **Softly** is to go   _______

    a. fast

    b. little by little

    c. running

4. **Blood** is   _______

    a. black

    b. red

    c. yellow

5. **Tracks** are made by   _______

    a. mud and water

    b. a thing that died

    c. a spook

Comprehension: YES or NO

1. Kim did think that Beth would go with them. _________

2. Nick and Dan went into the swamp without Beth and Kim. _________

3. Beth wanted to go to the old house. _________

4. The kids went from rock to rock to get to the house. _________

5. Dan went upstairs. _________

Fill-in-the-Blanks

blood   **spook**   **pools**   **tracks**   **door**

1. Dan said the cry was that of the old man's _____________.

2. The water in the swamp was in big _____________.

3. The kids saw mud _______________.

4. Nick and Dan ran out the _______________.

5. On Nick's hand there was _______________.

Chapter Study

What do you think of Nick now? ____

____

Why do you think that? ____

____

Prediction

What will the kids find when they go back into the house? ___________________________

____

____

The Old House
Chapter Four

Word Study: Pick one

1. Beth would run for help if things got **out of hand.** That is   ______

    a. Musty

    b. Cool

    c. Bad

2. A **room** is   ______

    a. A thing with water

    b. A spot on the block

    c. A spot with walls and a door

3. The tracks led to the **next** room. That is   ______

    a. The little room

    b. The room after

    c. The big room

4. Dan pushed the door just a **crack**.   ______

    a. A little

    b. A lot

    c. Not at all

5. It was like looking into a **black pool**.   ______

    a. Lots of sun

    b. No sun

    c. A crack

Comprehension: YES or NO

1. Kim would run for help if things got "out of hand". _________

2. There were lots of cracks in the walls upstairs. _________

3. There was blood on the rag at the end of the room. _________

4. Nick said they had to go back into the house. _________

5. Kim ran into the wall. _________

Fill-in-the-Blanks

crying   pool   room   bed   swooped

1. The track of blood spots led to a ______________.

2. They saw rags that had been made into a ______________.

3. "A man would not be ______________," said Dan.

4. The crash spooked the bats and they ______________.

5. It was so black in the room it was like a black ______________.

Character Study

What do you think of Beth now?____

____

Why do you think that? ____

____

Prediction

What do you think is at the spot next to the wall?________________________________

____

What will the kids do now?____

____

Name _______________________

Word Study: Pick one

1. The little kid was **<u>thin</u>**. _______

    a. Not fat

    b. Fat

    c. Big

2. Beth got **<u>food for Ted</u>**. _______

    a. Bats

    b. Fog

    c. A lunch

3. Dan **<u>jumped in</u>** fast. _______

    a. Said

    b. Went

    c. Came

4. He had **<u>nowhere</u>** to run. _______

    a. A spot

    b. No spot

    c. A room

5. I can tell by looking at them they are **<u>in a mess</u>**. _______

    a. Mad

    b. Musty

    c. Upset

Comprehension: YES or NO

1. The kids took Ted to Kim's house. __________

2. Ted wanted food. __________

3. Ted's house was at the back of the swamp. __________

4. Ted went to the next room and shut the door. __________

5. Beth's mom helped with the cut on Ted's hand. __________

Fill-in-the-Blanks

door   **next**   **run**   **dusk**   **softly**

1. Kim sat down ________________ to Ted.

2. When Ted got to the house it was ________________.

3. Ted went to the next room and shut the ________________.

4. He wanted to get out of there but had nowhere to ________________.

5. Ted said ________________ that he would not go back into the swamp.

Character Study

What do you think Ted is like? ______________________________________

____

Why? ____

____

Prediction

What do you think the kids' folks will do to the kids for going into the swamp?

____

____

What A Day
Chapter One

Name ___________________

Word Study: Pick One

1. She did not think of all the **trouble**.   _______

    a) a raft

    b) a lunch

    c) the mess

2. They made a **raft**.   _______

    a) a thing for food

    b) a thing to sit on in the water

    c) a thing that looks black

3. Nick did **flips**.   _______

    a) swoop up and down

    b) run and jump

    c) go up and over and over

4. Lunch was **packed**.   _______

    a) pushed on a raft

    b) pushed in a bag

    c) pushed up

5. Beth would **not last** down in the water.   _______

    a) die

    b) go out

    c) pushed up

Comprehension: YES or NO

1. The kids' folks were upset with them. _________

2. The kids made a raft. _________

3. Dan did lots of tricks in the water. _________

4. It began to rain. _________

5. Beth came up out of the water. _________

Fill-in-the-Blanks

rock   yet   lake   swimming   black

1. Nick was the best at _______________.

2. They pushed the raft onto a _______________.

3. It was cool by the _______________.

4. The water looked _______________.

5. The kids wanted the best day _______________.

Character Study

In this chapter I think Nick is ____.

I think that because____

____

____

Prediction:

What do you think will happen?____

____

____

What A Day
Chapter Two

Name _______________________

Word Study: Pick one

1. The kids **dragged** Beth.   ______

    a) pushed

    b) stopped

    c) pulled

2. Beth **blacked out**.   ______

    a) looked up

    b) sat up

    c) could not think

3. Beth wanted to **rest** a little.   ______

    a) stop

    b) swim

    c) yell

4. Stuff was **bobbing** on the water.   ______

    a) going in and out

    b) going up and down

    c) coming in

5. Nick said he could swim out there with no **trouble**.   ______

    a) plan

    b) push

    c) work

Comprehension: YES or NO

1. Dan could swim well. _________

2. Beth hit a rock when she fell. _________

3. Kim kept yelling. _________

4. Beth's skin was red. _________

5. A cry came from the stuff out on the lake. _________

Fill-in-the-Blanks

raining.   bobbing   rubbing   softly   bigger

1. Lots of stuff was _________________ on the water.

2. Beth said _______________ that they had all the trouble they wanted.

3. It was still _______________.

4. Kim kept _______________ Beth's hands.

5. Some of the stuff in the water was _______________ than the raft.

Character Study

What do you think of Kim in this chapter? _____________________________________

____

Why do you think that?____

____

____

Prediction

What is the stuff on the water and how did it get there?

____

____

What A Day
Chapter Three

Name _______________________

Word Study: Pick one

1. The **<u>rest of the kids</u>** could not swim well.   ______

    a) all the kids but Kim

    b) all the kids but Nick

    c) all the kids but Dan

2. Beth was not **<u>up to it</u>**.   ______

    a) not big

    b) not fast

    c) not well

3. Nick saw a **<u>mast</u>**.   ______

    a) stuff from a rock

    b) stuff from a ship

    c) a spook

4. Water made the mast **<u>tip</u>**.   ______

    a) flip

    b) trip

    c) crash

5. The girl was **<u>sobbing</u>**.   ______

    a) bobbing

    b) thinking

    c) crying

Comprehension: YES or NO

    1. Nick jumped into the water before the kids could stop him. _________

    2. The kids wanted Nick to come back to the raft. _________

    3. Nick could get into trouble out there by himself. _________

    4. Nick saw a kids hand resting on the water. _________

    5. Nick was wishing he had help. _________

Fill-in-the-Blanks

    mast   **blood**   **there**   **soon**

    1. Nick was way out in the water ________________.

    2. Kim wanted to get the raft out ________________.

    3. At last, Nick got to the ________________.

    4. The man's hand had lots of ________________ on it.

    5. Nick dragged the little girl up to the ________________.

Character Study:

In this chapter, Nick is ____

I think that because____

____

Prediction:

What do you think will happen and why do you think that?___________________________

____

____

What A Day
Chapter Four

Name ___________________________

Word Study: Pick one

1. The raft **left** the rock.   _____

   a) went to

   b) went away from

   c) pushed

2. They **hung** onto the raft.   _____

   a) held onto

   b) took

   c) helped

3. Stuff was **bobbing** in the water. _____

   a) kicking

   b) trapping

   c) going up and down

4. They went into the water in a **flash**. _____

   a) little by little

   b) fast

   c) soon

5. "I am **not well**", Beth was thinking. _____

   a) cross

   b) sick

   c) still

Comprehension: YES or NO

1. The kids could see Nick in the water. _________
2. The water helped push the raft out to Nick. _________
3. The kids got on the raft to rest. _________
4. The kids wanted to stay with the raft and Bob. _________
5. The water pushed the raft and the kids down. _________

Fill-in-the-Blanks

Dan   **The kids**   **Bob**   **Beth**   **Nick**

1. ________________ said, " Kim and I will stay in the water".
2. ________________ still felt sick from being in the water.
3. ________________ could not be seen.
4. ________________ could not stop Bob from jumping in the water
5. ________________ was saying, "Bob you are soooooo…"

Character study

What did you find out about Bob in this chapter and what do you think about him now?

____

____

Prediction

Beth was thinking, " What are we going to do now?" What do you think? _______________

____

____

Name ___________________________

Word Study: Pick one

1. "We must **<u>stay cool</u>**"… said Dan.   ______

     a) get upset

     b) get cross

     c) not get upset

2. The kids all saw the **<u>mast</u>**.   ______

     a) some of a house

     b) some of a raft

     c) some of a ship

3. He looked **<u>odd</u>**.   ______

     a) good

     b) sad

     c) messed up

4. The man **<u>blacked out</u>**.   ______

     a) went blank

     b) looked odd

     c) was upset

5. They got back **<u>to land</u>**.   ______

     a) off the raft

     b) off the water

     c) to the black

Comprehension: YES or NO

1. Stuff was bobbing in the water. _________

2. Nick yelled back. _________

3. Nick was on the mast of the ship. _________

4. Dan and Bob helped the girl on to the mast. _________

5. Bob and Dan ran for help. _________

Fill-in-the-Blank

Kim's mom   **Nick**   **The kids**   **The man**   **Bob and Dan**

1. _________________ got off the raft and pushed it.

2. "How can you get into all this trouble"? asked _______________.

3. _________________ lay still.

4. As they got to the raft, _________________ did not say a thing.

5. _________________ were in trouble with their folks.

Character Study

What do you think Nick will be like from now on? Why?_______________________

____

____

Prediction

What trouble do you think will find the kids next?

____

____

The Junk Yard
Chapter One

Name ___________________

1. Inference: Circle the ones that are true

Kim seems to be:

a thinker   troubled   funny   a planner

upset   sick   odd   in a mess

2. Main idea and details

What is the main idea of the chapter?______________________________________

Give two details that show this is true.

a.____

____

b.____

____

3. Sequencing

1. What did the dog do first when it was hit?________________________________

2. What did the dog do next? ____

After it got up what did it do?____

4. Cause and Effect

    1. What effect did the dog have on Kim?_______________________________________

    2. Why was the dog's leg hurt?____

    3. Why was Kim mad at herself?____

5. Inference and Critical Thinking

Why do you think Kim went to the junkyard? _________________________________

____

6. Predicting outcome.

What do you think will happen next? ____

____

____

Why do you think that? ____

____

____

The Junk Yard
Chapter Two

Name _______________________

1. What is the main idea of this chapter?_______________________________________

2. Give two details from the chapter that show why you think that?

____

____

____

____

____

3. **Cause and Effect:** Fill-in-the-Blank

Dan wanted the girls to play pool because _______________________________________

____

The kids made a pact because _______________________________________

Kim wanted to get rich so _______________________________________

4. **Inference:** Circle the things that are true.

   The kids felt badly about the trouble they had in the past so they:

made a pact   e) stayed away from trouble spots

helped plan for things   f) helped their folks

kept away from kids   g) did what their folks said

helped each other

5. **Sequencing**

Where was Beth at first in the chapter?____

Where did she go next?____

Where did she go last?____

6. **Context Clues:** Check the ones that are true.

In this chapter we see that…

______ The kids want to stay out of trouble.

______ The kids want to help each other stay out of trouble.

______ The kids folks are still upset.

______ Beth's mom is cross.

7. Do you think Beth will go to the junk yard?________________________________

Why do you think that?

____

____

____

The Junk Yard
Chapter Three

Name _______________________

Main Idea and Details

What is the main idea of this chapter?_______________________________________

____

Give two details from the chapter to show this.

a) ____

____

b) ____

____

Sequencing

Kim wanted to stop the dog in this chapter? What did Kim try first? _______________

____

What did she try next?____

____

At last what did she try?____

____

Cause and Effect

What did the dog do when Kim spoke softly?___________________________________

____

What spooked the dog?____

What made the dog mad? ____

Inference: Check all the things that are true.

The dog is…

____ good at it's job   ____does not like it's job   ____wanted to get at Kim

____ a thinker   ____felt trapped   ____was glad when Kim fell

____ kept it's cool

Critical Thinking
Why do you think this dog is good at it's job? ________________________________

____

____

____

Predicting Outcome

What will happen next?____

____

Why do you think that? ____

____

____

The Junk Yard
Chapter Four

Name ___________________

1. **Word Study:** Match

a) It would be faster if we **split up**.   1) could not think what to do

b) Sometimes people **pitch things**.   2) stop it

c) "**Cut it** out".   3) left

d) They **felt lost**.   4) some go this way other's go that way

e) They **took off**.   5) throw away

2) **Main Idea**

What is the main idea of the chapter?____

Show this by two details.

a.____

____

b.____

____

3. **Causes and Effect**

Nick will not play pool with Dan and Bob because_________________________

____

Beth is upset because____

____

They went to the junk yard because_______________________________________

4. Critical Thinking

What did the kids find odd? ____

Why did they think it was odd?____

How can you tell these kids like one another?_______________________________

____

5. Predicting Outcome

Do you think that the kids will stop the dog?________________________________

Why or why not? ____

____

____

Name ____________________

1. Inference

a) The dog could not think of what to do because_______________________________

____

b) The man that ran the junk yard yelled at the kids because ____________________

____

c) The kids did not think Kim was in the yard because ________________________

____

d) Nick told the man about Kim because _____________________________________

____

e) The man was thinking something was up because______________________________

____

2. Character Study

Tell two things about the man

a) _______________________________Why do you think that? _________________

____

b) _______________________________Why do you think that?_________________

____

3. Main Idea

a) The main idea of this chapter? _______________________________________

b) What makes you think that?

    1) ____

    2) ____

4. Sequence: Number the things as they were in the chapter

_____ The man yelled at the kids to not come back.

_____ The dog grabbed Kim's leg

_____ The man came to the yard and saw the kids.

_____ Nick told the man about Kim.

_____ The dog began licking Kim's hand.

_____ "Kim," they all yelled.

5. Critical Thinking

What do you think the kids would have done if the man had not come back to the

yard?

____

____

____

____

Name_______________________________

1. **Main Idea and Details**

    a)   What is the main idea in this chapter? _______________________________

    b)   What two details show this?

        1) ____

        ____

        2) ____

        ____

2. **Inference:** Check all things that show that the kids do not always get along.

- "The money is not yours," said Nick
- "We'll see what the boys think you should do," said Beth
- "We'll have lunch," said Dan.
- "I did find it so I can keep it," said Kim.
- "It's not yours, Kim," said Nick
- Maybe they can pool their money.
- "They should just keep out of it," Kim was thinking.

3. **Character Study:** Underline all things that seem true

Kim seem to feel…

sad   **happy**   **good**   **cross**   **upset**

trapped   **mad**   **badly**   **odd**

4. **Cause and Effect**

   1.   The kids could get lunch because _______________________________

   2.   Bob said Kim should keep the money because ____________________

   3.   The kids said someone must be looking for it because ______________

5. **Predicting Outcome**

What do you think Kim will do?

____

____

____

What will the other kids do if she does that?

____

____

____

Who do you think lost the money?

____

____

____

Name_______________________________

1.   **Sequencing:** Number the things as they were in the chapter

______   The kids left the mall.

______   Nick said they should get the cops help.

______   Kim took the money back to the shop.

______   Dan saw the man when he looked back.

______   Kim saw the big man by the shop.

______   Dan told Nick about seeing the man.

2.   **Critical Thinking**

a)   Why do you think the man is on the kids' block?

____

____

b)   List two things you think the boys should do?

____

____

3.   **Context Clues**

a)   The kids help when they find trouble. What are two things in the chapter that show this?

____

b)   What do you think Kim will be like when she gets home?

____

4.   **Cause and Effect**

a)   Why did Kim take the money to the shop?

____

b)   Why is the man coming after the kids?

____

c)   Why did Bob say not to tell their folks?

____

5.   **Predicting Outcome**

a) What will the boys do?

____

____

b) What will Kim do when she gets home?

____

____

c) What will the man do next?

____

____

At The Mall

Chapter Three

Name_________________________________

1.   **Facts: Match**

     1. The folks made a pact   a) that he did a good job

     2. Nick spotted the man   b) just down the block from Kim

     3. The man hid   c) at Kim's house

     4. Nick's mom was happy   d) to not get mad

     5. The kids were having fun   e) behind some bushes

2.   **Context Clues:** In this chapter we see that: (Check all)

- The man wants the money.
- The boys are not too upset.
- Lots of kids hang out on the block.
- The girls were upset.
- The boy's plan was a good one.
- Nick is a good thinker.
- The kids are in big trouble.

3.   **Cause and Effect**

1. The man was on the block because

____

2. Nick ran after the man because

____

3. Nick was winded because

____

4. List two things you think about the man in this chapter.

    a. ____

    b. ____

4.   Predicting

a. How will Nick be when he gets to Kim's?

____

____

b. What will the man do next?

____

____

c. What will the kids do next?

____

____

d. Will the man at the shop give Kim the money? _______________

  Why do you think that?

____

____

1. Critical Thinking

a) Why didn't Dan and Bob say anything when Nick told them what happened with the man?

____

____

b) What do you think Nick is like after the man grabbed him?

____

____

c) Why do you think that?

____

____

d) List two things you think about Dan's plan to tell the girls that someone came for the money.

____

____

e) Nick, Dan and Bob all had a plan. What plan can you think of?

____

____

f) Do you think Kim would go back for the money if they told her about the man?

____

Why? ____

2. Predicting Outcome: Match

1. The girls will likely   a) stay back

2. The man will likely   b) still have the money

3. The boys will likely   c) see the man and come back

4. The shop man will likely   d) run to try to stop the girls

5. Someone will likely   e) have come for the money

3. Inference:

Check 6 of the ways the kids were thinking of doing with the money.

- Things to wear
- Trips
- A farm
- A snake
- Things for the folks
- A ship
- A horse
- A house
- CD's
- Food
- A pool
- A trunk
- Trees

Will Kim or the man end up with the money? ______________________________

Why do you think that?

____

____

Name___________________________

1. Main Idea and Details

a. What is the main idea of this chapter?

____

b. Give two details why you think that?

____

____

2. Sequence

a. When Kim came out of the shop with the money, what did the man do first?

____

b. What did he do next?

____

c. Then what did he do?

____

d. At last what stopped him?

____

3. Cause and Effect: Match

1. Maybe the man left because   a) Kim's mom got them.

2. The cops came because   b) the boys took off running

3. Kim's mom got the cops because   c) he did not think the kids would go back for the money

4. The kids' folks wanted   d) school to begin

5. The kids' folks came to the   e) she was thinking of the money
   Mall because

6. Kim did not see the man because   f) they felt the kids were in trouble

7. Kim left for the mall in lots of   g) she wanted the money
   time because

4. Character Study: These books have 5 kids in them.
   Pick three of them that you liked best and tell why you liked them.

Nick, Dan, Kim, Bob, Beth

__________   ______________________________________

                   ____

                   ____

__________   ______________________________________

                   ____

                   ____

__________   ______________________________________

                   ____

A	B	C	D	E	F	G	H
Added	Back	Came	Day	End	Farm	Gate	Hand
After	Badly	Cobweb	Die		Farmer	Gave	Hay
Again	Bank	Colours	Died		Fast	Get	Help
All	Barn	Come	Dim		Faster	Girls	Head
Are	Because	Cool	Dirty		Fell	Going	Her
Asked	Before	Could	Door		Felt	Good	Herself
Away	Began	Crash	Don't		Find	Grabbed	Here
	Best	Cross	Down		Five		Horse
	Better	Cry	Dragged		Flash		House
	Black	Crying	Dripping		Flip		Hugged
	Blood	Cut	Duck		Folks		Hurt
	Bobbing		Dusk		Food		
	Boot				From		
	Boss				Funny		
	Boys						
	Bush						
	Bushes						
	By						

J	K	L	M	N	O	P	R
Job	Keep	Lake	Making	Next	Odd	Pack	Raft
Jug	Kept	Land	Mast	Not	Oh	Pact	Rain
Junk	Kicked	Last	May	Nod	On	Path	Rest
Just	Kicking	Lay	Maybe	Noon	One	Pass	Ribs
Jump	Kid	Led	Mess	Now	Onto	Past	Ride
Jumping	Kill	Left	Money		Open	Pay	Riding
	Killer	Let's	More		Opened	Picked	Ring
		Lick	Much		Out	Pit	Rock
		Like	Mud		Over	Play	Room
		Little	Must			Pool	Running
		Lock	Musty			Pushed	
		Locked				Put	
		Lost					
		Lunch					

S	S	S	T	T	U	W	W
Said	Sky	Spot	Take	Top	Upstairs	Wall	When
Sand	Slept		Tell	Tools	Use	Want	Who
Saw	Slow		That	Track		Was	Why
Sell	Slowly		There	Trick		Water	Win
Seen	Smash		Their	Trapped		Wave	Wind
She	Sobbing		There	Trees		Waving	Work
Shed	Softly		Thin	Tripped		Way	Would
Ship	Some		Thing	Trouble		Wear	
Shot	Soon		Think	Trunk		Well	
Should	Smell		This	Try		Were	
Shut	Snake		Time			Wet	
Sick	Split		Told			Where	
Skin	Spook		Took			What	

New Start Suspense Series - Part 1

**The Swamp The Old House What A Day The
Junk Yard The Trip
At The Mall**

New Start Suspense Series

"I can't read." "I'm dumb." "I'm stupid, stupid, stupid!"

Many people with reading difficulties, are feeling this way and expressing these thoughts. The reasons are as varied as the individuals.
Remedies for this situation have been limited until now. These people need a new start. It is for these individuals that the New Start Suspense Series has been written.

Patnor Publishing
242 First Ave. North, Unit 204 Welland, Ontario, Canada   L3C 7J2

www.patnorpublishing.com

ISBN 0-9733663-7-0